EVERYDAY INVENTIONS

Get the Message

Jane Bidder

W
FRANKLIN WATTS
LONDON • SYDNEY

First published in 2006 by
Franklin Watts

Franklin Watts
338 Euston Road
London NW1 3BH

Franklin Watts Australia
Level 17/207 Kent Street
Sydney
NSW 2000

Series editor: Jennifer Schofield
Designer: Ross George
Picture researcher: Diana Morris
Artwork: Ray Bryant
Photography: Ray Moller unless otherwise acknowledged

Acknowledgements:
The author would like to thank Mary Bellis
of http://inventors.about.com for her help
in researching this book.

AKG Images: 10t, 14, 19; Alex Bartel/SPL: 7b; Bettmann/Corbis: 16, 21, 23t,
27b; British Library/HIP Topfoto: 7t ; Corbis: 18bl; Steve Crise/Corbis: 11;
Julio Donoso/Sygma/Corbis: 26; Mary Evans Picture Library: 10b, 12b;
Alexander Farnsworth/IW/Topfoto:23b; LWA-JDC/Corbis: 24; Museum of
London/HIP/Topfoto: 9c; Richard T Nowitz/Corbis: 27t; Courtesy of Phillips:
3c, 3b, 4t, 12t, 20t, 22t; Picturepoint/Topfoto: 9b, 22b; Louie Psihoyos/Corbis: 25;
RNT Productions/Corbis: 18tr; Roger-Viollet/Topfoto: 20b.

Every attempt has been made to clear copyright. Should there be any
inadvertent omission please apply to the publisher for rectification.

The author would like to dedicate this book to her children
William, Lucy and Giles.

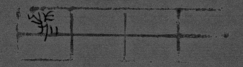

Contents

About inventions   4

The printed word   6

Postal services   8

Electric telegraph   10

The telephone   12

Pens   14

Photography   16

Cinema   18

Radio   20

Television   22

The Internet   24

Other inventions   26

Timeline   28

Glossary   30

Websites   31

Index   32

About inventions

An invention is a device or gadget that is designed and made for the first time. The person who makes the device is called an inventor. In this book, we look at inventions that help us to stay in contact with each other and communicate our ideas and thoughts. We look at who invented these gadgets and how they have changed over time.

Easy living

Many gadgets have been invented because people want to improve their lives or make them easier. For example, ball-point pens are much easier to write with and carry around than fountain pens. Their invention in 1935 meant that people no longer had to refill their pens constantly or suffer from ink splodges on paper, or even on themselves!

Getting it right first time

Some inventors have an idea and work hard to make their invention work. For example, in 1827, the French scientist, Joseph Niepce, was working with light. He was trying to find a quicker way to capture images than drawing. Niepce did find a way to capture images as he made the first photograph.

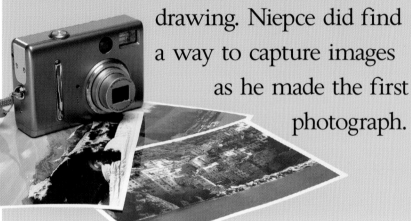

TIMELINES

You will find timelines throughout this book. They show in date order when a specific breakthrough or invention occurred.

Sometimes the dates are very exact, but other times they point to a particular era, for example the late 1960s.

Use these timelines to keep track of when things happened.

From one, comes another

Not all inventions are thought of instantly - many of them develop from other inventions. For example, the first telephones required a telephone wire for each person you wanted to contact. Then the telephone exchange was invented, but you had to call the operator to be connected. Now you can dial straight through or use your mobile phone almost wherever you are.

The printed word

We read and write every day but people have not always known how to do this. Writing was invented

by people living in Mesopotamia (modern-day Iraq) about 5,500 years ago. From that time onwards, writing has developed. People have learnt how to make paper and how to print words.

Woodblock printing

In about 700 CE, the Chinese invented woodblock printing. Letters were carved out of blocks of wood and their surface was covered with ink. The printer then pressed these blocks down onto a piece of paper so that the letters were 'printed' on the page.

Making paper
In 2500 BCE, Egyptians made paper from papyrus reeds gathered from river banks. Today, paper is made mostly from wood pulp.

Printing press

In 1440, Johannes Gutenberg from Germany invented a printing press that could print around 3,000 pages a day. Before this, books had to be copied by hand. To print a page, metal letters were arranged line-by-line, covered in ink and then printed onto the paper. The letters could be reused many times.

Today's printing presses

Today, most printing presses use a method of printing called lithography. This uses printing plates to press words and pictures onto the

paper passing under the press. The biggest presses can print, trim and fold 80,000 copies of a 96-page newspaper in an hour.

TIMELINE

3500 BCE
Writing is invented.

700 CE
The Chinese print with woodblocks.

1040-50
The Chinese invent moveable type.

1440
Gutenberg invents the printing press and prints a Bible.

1719
People start to print in colour.

1798
Alois Senefelder from Germany develops lithographic printing.

1938
America's Chester Carlson invents a printing process called electrophotography which is the basis for today's laser printers.

1971
The first laser printer is made by Xerox.

Postal services

Each day, all over the world, postmen and postwomen deliver letters and parcels to people's homes. However, the postal service is not new - it was started as long ago as 1464.

Royal post

The first postal service is said to have been started in 1464 by French King Louis XI. In 1516, Henry VIII of England set up a postal service for the delivery of royal mail only. Messengers on horseback and young postboys on foot delivered this mail. Then, in 1635, everyone was allowed to use the royal mail service, so long as they paid for it.

Postboxes
The first street postboxes were not very successful. People often posted their litter, making the boxes a haven for rats!

Mail coaches

Mail coaches replaced postboys in the 18th century. With improvements to their design, horse-drawn coaches could speed along and carry a lot of mail. However, it was very expensive to send a letter by royal mail.

Stamps

The Englishman Sir Rowland Hill wanted to create a good postal service that everyone could afford to use. In 1840, he came up with the idea of using a stamp to cover the cost of postage, regardless of where the letter was going in the UK. Seven years later, the USA created a 5-cent postage stamp with a picture of Benjamin Franklin on it.

TIMELINE

1464
King Louis XI starts a postal service.

1516
Henry VIII sets up a royal mail service.

1635
Everyone is allowed to use the royal mail.

1700s
High-speed mail coaches start crossing America and England.

Late 1700s
Mail coaches become much faster.

1840
Sir Rowland Hill invents the first stamp called the Penny Black.

1847
The first US stamp is made.

1860
The Pony Express postal service begins in the USA but it is soon overtaken by the telegraph.

Electric telegraph

The electric telegraph is a communications system that sends messages by an electric pulse to a receiving station. Over the years, telegraphs have been used to send messages from ships at sea and between soldiers at war.

A code that worked

The pulses of electricity used to send telegraphs create a series of dots and dashes on a roll of paper at the receiving end. The dots and dashes, which represent letters and numbers, are then decoded. The dots and dashes are called Morse code. Morse code was invented in 1835 by Samuel Morse and Alfred Vail of the USA.

The first telegraph message

Morse and Vail went on to develop the telegraph, which they showed to government officials in the USA, in 1838. However, it was another four years before they persuaded the government to fund their invention. Then they built a telegraph wire to link Washington to Baltimore, 65 kilometres away. It worked. The first message it sent on 24 May 1844 was "What hath God wrought."

Using telegraph lines

From 1845, the lines used to send telegraph messages were also used to send telegrams. Telegrams were printed telegraph messages, delivered as fast as possible by special postboys. Then, in 1971, e-mail was invented and telegrams lost popularity.

TIMELINE

1835
Morse code is invented by Samuel Morse and Alfred Vail.

1844
The first telegraph message is sent by Morse and Vail.

1845
Telegraph wires are used to send telegrams.

1858
A telegraph cable is laid under the Atlantic, but it only works for one month.

1866
A second transatlantic cable is laid, which continues to work to this day.

1971
E-mail is invented.

The telephone

Today, across the world, there are millions of landline and mobile telephones in use. However, when the telephone was first invented, people were not sure that it would even catch on.

Marvellous Meucci

Many people think that Alexander Graham Bell invented the first telephone in 1876. However, it is now believed that an Italian-American called Antonio Meucci (right) discovered that sound travelled down a copper wire in 1849. Over the next 30 years he worked on his invention but never had enough money to make it a success. Bell developed the same idea in 1876 to create the first telephone.

The telephone exchange

With the first telephones you had to call an operator to be put through to a number. An American, Almon Strowger, realised that his business was losing out because people kept being put through to his rivals. So, in 1891, he invented the automatic telephone exchange. This allowed people to dial direct without an operator.

Mobile madness

In 1978, trials for the first mobile telephone began. Speech travelled along invisible radio waves, rather than along telephone cables. At first these telephones were expensive and not many people owned one, but as technology has improved, they have become cheaper and more efficient.

TIMELINE

1849
Antonio Meucci invents the concept of the telephone.

1876
Alexander Graham Bell develops Meucci's idea for a telephone.

1891
Almon Strowger invents the first telephone exchange.

1978
Mobile telephones are first tested.

2000s
Mobile phones become a way for people to keep in touch in isolated areas, such as parts of Africa.

2006
Nokia launches the N92 mobile telephone. It is one of the first mobiles on which you can watch television.

Pens

Using a pen to scribble on a piece of paper is one of the easiest ways to get a message to someone, to make a note for yourself and to record information. Today, pens come in all shapes and sizes, but this was not always the case.

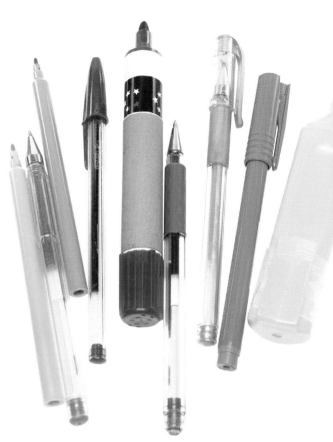

Quill pens

Records show that people living in Europe as long ago as 700 CE used birds' feathers to make pens called quills. They sharpened the tip of the feather to make a fine point and then dipped it in ink to write with. Beautiful handwriting was much admired.

Fountain pens

In the 18th century, France's Nicholas Bion designed one of the first fountain pens. A fountain pen has a store of ink inside the pen which flows down to the nib. Although these pens were better than quills, they spilled a lot of ink. In 1884, the USA's Lewis Waterman developed a pen that had a hole above the nib and three grooves inside to help the ink flow better.

Ball-point pens

In 1938, a pair of Hungarian brothers, Ladislas and Georg Biro, invented a pen with a tiny ball as its writing point. The ball helped the ink to flow smoothly and gave the pen its name. Today, ball-point pens remain one of the most popular types of pen.

TIMELINE

3500 BCE
Mesopotamians use a reed pen to record information on clay.

3000 BCE
Egyptians write with a reed pen on papyrus.

100 CE
Romans write using a metal stick, called a stylus, on a wax tablet.

700-1800 CE
Quill pens are used.

1709
Nicholas Bion invents the first fountain pen.

1884
Lewis Waterman improves the design of the fountain pen.

1938
The Biro brothers invent the ball-point pen, or biro.

1960s
The first felt-tip pen is invented.

Photography

Can you imagine reading a newspaper or magazine with no photographs in it, or going on a holiday and not taking a single picture to remember it by?

The first photograph

In 1827, a French scientist called Joseph Niepce made the first photograph. He attached a lens to a wooden box and placed a metal plate covered in a layer of tar inside. The lens projected

a picture onto the tar. Where light from the lens hit the tar, it hardened. After eight hours, Niepce washed away the soft tar, to reveal the photograph above.

Kodak Number 1

In 1888, George Eastman of the USA invented the first hand-held camera. The camera was called the Kodak Number 1 and it was similar to today's disposable cameras. When you had used all the film, you sent the camera back to the makers who printed the photos for you.

Polaroid

Polaroid cameras were invented in 1947 by Edwin Land. This camera was different because as soon as you had clicked the button, a developing photograph appeared. At first Polaroids were really expensive, but as more people used them, they became cheaper.

TIMELINE

1827
Joseph Niepce makes the first photograph.

1837
Louis Daguerre invents a much better photographic process.

1850
William Henry Fox Talbot invents the modern photographic process.

1861
The first colour photograph is taken.

1888
George Eastman invents a small hand-held camera.

1935
Kodak sells colour film.

1947
Polaroid cameras are first sold.

1984
Canon invents the still digital camera.

Cinema

Moving pictures hit the big screen as long ago as 1895. They were different from today's films. However, they still worked in the same way by showing sequences of still pictures so fast that they appeared to move.

Early beginnings

In 1891 William Dickson, who worked with Thomas Edison, made a camera that took 46 photographs each second. Edison then made the kinetoscope. It had a peep hole through which people could see Dickson's flickering images. Later, Edison developed the kinetoscope to make a film projector.

Screen machine

The first machine to show a projected film was invented in 1895 in France, by Auguste and Louis Lumière. Their invention, called the Cinematographe, was used to show films on a screen in a darkened room, similar to today's cinema.

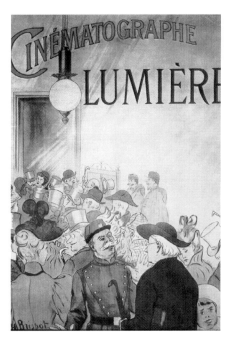

Adding sound and colour

At first, films were not only short but they were also in black and white and silent. The only sound was provided by a pianist. Then, in 1927, *The Jazz Singer* was made. It was one of the first films made with synchronised sound. This meant that the film's sound, including talking, was heard at the same time as the picture was shown on the screen.

T I M E L I N E

1891
Dickson makes the first moving pictures.

1895
The Cinematographe is invented by the Lumière brothers.

1900
The first films with sound are made.

1903
The first western *The Great Train Robbery* is made in America.

1914
Picture palaces, or movie houses, were built in Britain.

1917
The first true-colour movies are made.

1927
The first film with synchronised sound is screened.

1967
The Imax 3-D system is invented in Canada.

Radio

Radios keep us in touch with the latest pop songs, news, weather and much more. Have you ever wondered how the information reaches your radio? The radio station sends out radio waves carrying information that your radio receives and turns into music or speech.

Marconi's magic

The inventor who really made radio possible was an Italian living in Britain called Guglielmo Marconi. In 1895, Marconi sent a Morse code (see page 10) message across a room, without using wires. He went on to improve his discovery.

Words and music

Marconi's invention could send only Morse code messages between two people. But in 1906, Reginald Fessenden of the USA discovered how to broadcast (send) words and music on radio waves, much to the surprise of people listening in. Radio broadcasting had begun.

Radio stations

By 1920, radio stations had sprung up all over the USA. In Britain, only the BBC was

allowed to broadcast and, at first, it was limited to a few hours a day. However, it was not long before listening to the radio became a family activity. Everyone sat around it in the evening, listening to programmes.

TIMELINE

1864
England's James Clerk Maxwell first gets the idea for radio.

1895
Guglielmo Marconi invents equipment that sends out radio waves, carrying a message to a receiver some distance away.

1901
Marconi sends a radio message across the Atlantic Ocean to Canada.

1906
Reginald Fessenden broadcasts sound and music.

1920s
Radio stations start in the USA and Britain.

1999
The first digital radios go on sale.

Television

Television provides people with news, entertainment and information. The TV receives a picture signal,  sent from the television station, through the TV aerial, satellite dish or a cable. It then builds up a picture in lines across the screen. Our eyes make all the lines join together to form a clear picture.

In England

In the 1920s, Scottish engineer, John Logie Baird, experimented with radio waves to see if he could send picture signals as well as sound signals along these invisible waves. In 1924, he managed to get an outline picture of an object on a screen. Two years later, he was able to demonstrate moving pictures.

In the United States

At about the same time, Philo Farnsworth of the USA had started his own experiments in producing images on a screen. In 1927, he is said to have shown a straight line on a television screen and later a puff of smoke.

Satellite television

Satellite television became popular in the 1980s. Today, you can see the satellite dishes that pick up the television signal on many houses and apartments. Satellite dishes pick up signals which are sent into space by television stations and bounced back to Earth off satellites.

TIMELINE

1924
John Logie Baird and Philo Farnsworth work on showing pictures on a television screen.

1928
Baird sends television pictures from England to America.

1936
In Britain, the British Broadcasting Corporation (BBC) shows its first TV programmes.

1960s
The first colour TV sets are produced.

1980s
Satellite television arrives.

2004
Recording systems are built into satellite transmitter boxes.

The Internet

The Internet is not only one of the fastest ways to find out information, but without it, e-mail would not be possible. E-mail is one of the quickest ways to send a message to someone.

How it all started

During the 1960s, scientists in the USA developed a computer network called SAGE. SAGE was used to link radar stations across the USA and was intended to provide early warning of a Russian attack. It never worked properly but scientists went on to develop a similar computer network, called ARPANET, linking the computers of various US Government Departments.

Safety first!
Never communicate with strangers on e-mail or in chat rooms. Check with an adult before you use the Internet for your homework.

Sending e-mails

In 1971, Ray Tomlinson, an American engineer, invented electronic mail or e-mail. Tomlinson used ARPANET to work out a way for researchers to send each other messages. He chose the @ symbol to show which network the person was using. Today, across the world, millions of e-mails are sent and received each day to addresses at work, schools and homes.

Web browsing

In 1990, Britain's Tim Berners-Lee created the first web browser. This computer program allowed the user to get into and download information from websites on a global computer network called the Internet.

1960s
SAGE is developed in the USA to act as an early warning system of attack during the Cold War.

Late 1960s
SAGE is developed to form ARPANET – an information-sharing computer program.

1971
Ray Tomlinson invents electronic mail (e-mail).

1990
Tim Berners-Lee creates the first web browser.

1998
Google, one of the biggest search engines, is created by Larry Page and Sergey Brin of the USA.

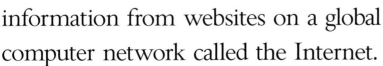

Other inventions

Each day, people use many other inventions to communicate their thoughts and ideas. For example, people who cannot see use Braille, a series of raised dots on a page, to read and write. A special sign language is also used by people who have hearing difficulties.

Braille

There are millions of people who cannot see. So that these people can read and keep in touch, a type of writing called Braille was invented by the Frenchman, Louis Braille, in 1824. Braille is a writing system that uses patterns of raised dots to represent letters or words. People read by feeling the shape of the pattern with their fingers. During the 1940s and 1950s, special Braille typewriters were also invented.

Signing

Signing is a system of hand signals and facial expressions that helps people communicate without talking. It is possible that signing first started

in the 18th century in France. There are different forms of sign language including American Sign Language and International Sign Language.

Mechanical telegraph

In 1792, the French Chappe brothers invented a machine that moved a pair of wooden arms in a particular pattern to represent letters of the alphabet. Their invention allowed messages to be sent from telegraph to telegraph. It also developed into a flag signalling system used by sailors, called semaphore.

In the 11th century BCE, the Phonecians (living around the Mediterranean) established a simple alphabet. It did not have vowels and it was only in about 900 BCE that the Greeks added them.

Later, the Etruscans (people from an acient state of Italy) and the Romans improved on this alphabet to make it the alphabet that we use today.

Timeline

3500 BCE
The Mesopotamians invent the first writing system.

1300 BCE
The Romans write using wax tablets and a stylus.

700 CE
Woodblock printing is used in China.

700-1800 CE
Quill pens are used throughout Europe.

1440
Gutenberg invents a printing press that uses moveable type and prints a Bible.

1516
A royal postal service starts in England.

1798
Alois Senefelder develops lithographic printing.

1824
Braille is invented.

1827
Niepce produces the first photograph.

1835
Morse code is invented.

1845
The first telegram is sent in Britain.

1840
The Penny Black is made.

1849
Meucci makes a discovery that leads to the telephone.

1850

William Fox Talbot develops photography in Britain.

1876

Alexander Graham Bell develops Meucci's idea for a telephone.

1888

George Eastman invents a small camera.

1891

Almon Strowger invents the first telephone exchange.

1895

The Cinematographe is made by the Lumière brothers.

1901

Marconi sends radio signals across the Atlantic Ocean.

1906

Sound and music is broadcast.

1920s

The television is invented.

1927

The first 'talking' film is shown.

1947

Polaroid cameras go on sale.

Late 1960s

The Internet is invented.

1971

Ray Tomlinson invents e-mail.

1978

Mobile telephones are tested.

1984

Canon invents the still digital camera.

Glossary

ARPANET
A computer network set up in the 1960s by the United States Department of Defense Advanced Research Projects Agency (ARPA).

Broadcast
A radio or television signal that is transmitted over a large area so that many people can receive it.

Cold War
The clash of ideas that developed after World War II between the United States and its allies and the Soviet Union and its allies.

Digital camera
A camera that does not use film. Once taken, the photographs can be viewed on the camera or they can be loaded onto a computer and printed out.

Isolated
Not near to anything.

Network
A group of linked communication devices such as telephones and computers.

Operator
The person who connects a telephone call to the person on the other end of the line.

Patented
When someone applies for and receives the rights to an invention. When an invention is patented, it cannot be copies by another inventor.

Project
To show a film on a big screen.

Radio wave
An electromagnetic wave that has a low frequency and long wavelength. Radio waves are used in both radio and television broadcasts.

Search engine
An Internet site that enables you to search the whole Internet.

Transatlantic
Crossing the Atlantic ocean.

Web browser
Computer software that organises pictures, text and sound into on-screen pages.

Websites

www.nationalgeographic.com/features/96/inventions
Have loads of fun with games about inventions.

http://home.howstuffworks.com
Find out how everyday inventions work by searching for them on this website.

www.makingthemodernworld.org.uk
Find out about the many inventions that have changed the way we live, work and entertain ourselves.

www.uspto.gov/web/offices/ac/ahrpa/opa/kids/index.html
Visit the American Patent and Trademark Office's website to find out more about inventions and how they are patented.

www.magic-factory.co.uk
Visit this fantastic interactive website to learn all there is to know about photography and taking snapshots.

www.connected-earth.com
Discover how the technology used for communication has changed and developed over time.

www.americanhistory.si.edu/cinema
Find out more about the history of motion pictures.

www.smithsonianassociates.org/programs/berners-lee/berners-lee.asp
Hear the inventor of the Internet, Tim Berners-Lee talking about his invention and how it has changed our lives.

Note to parents:
Every effort has been made by the publishers to ensure that the websites in this book are suitable for children, that they are of the highest educational value, and that they contain no inappropriate or offensive material. However, due to the nature of the Internet, it is impossible to guarantee that the contents of these sites will not be altered. We strongly advise that Internet access is supervised by a responsible adult.

Index

alphabets 27
ARPANET 24, 25, 30

Baird, John Logie 22, 23
BBC 21, 23, 29
Bell, Alexander Graham 12, 13, 29
Berners-Lee, Tim 25
Bion, Nicholas 15
Biro, Ladislas and George 15
Braille 26, 28
    Braille typewriters 26
Braille, Louis 26
broadcasts and broadcasting 21, 29, 30

cameras 17, 18, 29
    digital 17, 29, 30
    disposable 17
    Polaroid 17, 29
Chappe brothers 27
cinema 18-19, 29
Cinematographe 19, 29
Cold War 25

Daguerre, Louis 17
Dickson, William 18

Eastman, George 17, 29
Edison, Thomas 18
electric telegraph 10-11
e-mail 11, 24, 25, 29

Farnsworth, Philo 23
Fessenden, Reginald 21
Fox Talbot, William Henry 17, 28
Franklin, Benjamin 9

Google 25
Gutenberg, Johannes 7, 28

Hill, Rowland 9

Imax 19
ink 4, 6, 7, 14, 15
Internet 24-25, 29, 31

Jazz Singer, The 19

Kinetoscope 18, 30
Kodak Number 1 17

Land, Edwin 17
lithography 9
Louis XI 8, 9
Lumiere, Auguste and Louis 19, 29

Marconi, Guglielmo 20, 21, 29
Meucci, Antonio 12, 13, 28, 29
Morse code 10, 11, 20, 21, 28
Morse, Samuel 10, 11

newspapers 9, 16, 28
Niepce, Joseph 5, 16, 17, 28

operators 5, 13, 30

paper 6, 7, 14
papyrus 6, 15
Penny Black 9, 28
pens 4, 14-15
    ballpoint pens 4, 15
    felt-tip pens 15
    fountain pens 4, 15
    reed pens 15

photography 5, 16-17, 28, 29
Pony Express 9
postal services 8-9, 28
postboxes 8
printing 6-7, 17
printing plates 7

quills 14, 15, 28

radio 20-21
radio waves 13, 20, 21, 22, 30

SAGE 24, 25, 30
satellite television 23
search engine 25, 30
semaphore 27
Senefelder, Alois 7
sign language 26, 27
stamps 9, 28
Strowger, Almon 13, 29

telegrams 11, 28
telephone exchange 5, 13, 29
telephones 5, 11, 12-13
    mobile telephones 5, 12, 13, 17, 29
television 22-23, 29
Tomlinson, Ray 25, 29

Vail, Alfred 10, 11

Waterman, Lewis 15
wax tablets 15, 28
web browser 25, 30
woodblock printing 6, 7, 28
writing 6, 7, 26, 28